COG RAILWAY TO PIKE'S PEAK

◆

Morris W. Abbott

Golden West Books
San Marino, California · 91108

COG RAILWAY TO PIKE'S PEAK
Copyright © 1973 by Morris W. Abbott
All Rights Reserved
Published by Golden West Books
San Marino, California 91108 U.S.A.

ISBN No. 87095-052-5

First Printing — May 1973
Second Printing — May 1974
Third Printing — May 1975
Fourth Printing — August 1975
Fifth Printing — May 1976
Sixth Printing — August 1976
Seventh Printing — May 1977
Eighth Printing — May 1978
Ninth Printing — May 1979

Library of Congress Cataloging in Publication Data

Abbott, Morris W
   Cog railway to Pike's Peak.

   Shortened version of the author's Pike's Peak Cog
Road.
   1. Manitou and Pike's Peak Railway.   I.   Title.
TF688.P53A2 1973   385'.6'0978856   73-9520
ISBN 0-87095-052-5

THE COVER ILLUSTRATION

Boulders, boulders and more boulders! That is what the summit of Pike's Peak is like and it can't be expressed any better than in this picturesque scene as Swiss-built diesel-electric train No. 15 approaches the summit. — COURTESY OF COLORPICTURE PUBLISHERS, INC., BOSTON, MASSACHUSETTS

Golden West Books

A Division of Pacific Railroad Publications, Inc.

P.O. BOX 8136 • SAN MARINO, CALIFORNIA • 91108

COG RAILWAY TO PIKE'S PEAK

MORRIS W. ABBOTT

The Manitou & Pike's Peak Railway, commonly known as the Cog Road, has been carrying people to the summit of Pike's Peak in comfort and safety since 1891. It has the distinction of reaching the highest elevation above sea level of any rack railway in the world (14,110 feet), and its length of 8.9 miles is exceeded by only one, in Switzerland.

Pike's Peak looms 8,000 feet above the gateway rocks of the Garden of the Gods. The Cog Road is just over the crest of the mountain. — STEWARTS COMMERCIAL PHOTOGRAPHERS

Although Pike's Peak is not as high as a number of other mountains in Colorado, it is fortunately situated near the plains instead of being surrounded by other peaks. Because of this there are remarkable views in all directions from its summit, including downward.

3

Lt. Zebulon M. Pike, U.S. Army, sighted *The Great Peak* in 1806, while leading a party of 26 men on an exploratory journey through a part of the newly purchased Louisiana territory. Pike erroneously estimated the peak to be over 18,000 feet in elevation, and failed to reach its summit.

The Great Peak is what Lt. Zebulon M. Pike called it when he first sighted it in 1806. He not only failed to reach its top, but declared that man might never tread its summit. He estimated its elevation to be 18,581 feet, much of his error being due to his belief that the plains were 4,500 feet higher than they really are. In 1820, however, Dr. Edwin James, a member of Major Stephen H. Long's party of explorers, did climb to the top, and for some years after that the mountain was known as James Peak. A rude trail of sorts is said to have existed as early as 1852, and the first woman to conquer the mountain was Mrs. Julia A. Holmes in 1858. Her husband didn't make it.

In 1882 the summit house looked like this, and was a weather observatory for the U.S. Signal Service. — KOCH COLLECTION

The U.S. Signal Service (forerunner of today's National Weather Service) thought for a time that Pike's Peak would be an ideal location for a weather observatory, and accordingly in 1871 erected a sturdy stone house at its summit, laid out a trail via Bear Creek and Lake Moraine, and strung a single wire along it for telegraphic communication. In 1882 a shorter but steeper trail was built up Ruxton Creek from Manitou, along the route later followed by the Cog Road. The weather station was discontinued not many years later because it was found that the weather on the peak had little in common with that on the plains.

The first of several proposed railroads to the summit, and the only one beside the Manitou & Pike's Peak Railway that got past the planning stage, was the Pike's Peak Railway & Improvement Company, organized in 1883. Its goal was to build a narrow gauge line from Manitou to the summit via Crystal Park and the Seven Lakes. Stock was sold and several miles of the right-of-way were graded, but the company collasped when the bank in New York City failed to open its doors the very day after the company's money had been deposited in it.

The prime mover in the promotion of the Manitou & Pike's Peak Railway Company was Major John Hulbert of Manitou, who had the backing of other local businessmen as well as some mining and banking millionaires. The company was incorporated in 1888, financed entirely by Zalmon G. Simmons

Zalmon G. Simmons of Kenosha, Wisconsin, built the Cog Road (which he and his family owned until 1925) after an uncomfortable round trip to the summit on a mule. — DENVER PUBLIC LIBRARY, WESTERN COLLECTION

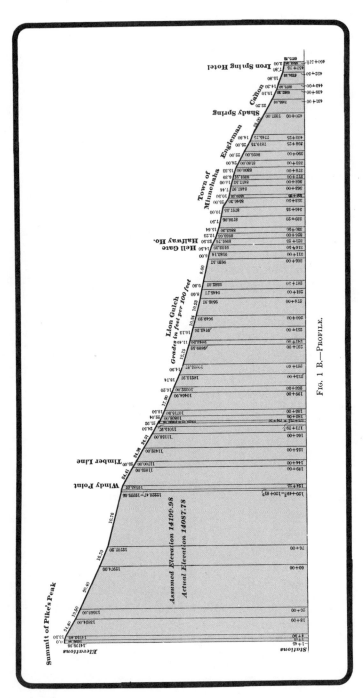

Fig. 1 B.—Profile.

This profile of the Manitou & Pike's Peak Railway was prepared by Thomas F. Richardson and appeared in the *Journal of the Association of Engineering Societies*. The first 25 percent grade is below Minnehaha, the next is Son-of-a-Gun Hill. The Big Hill ranges from 22.05 to 25 percent for a brief stretch, and in addition there is a short stretch of 24.4 percent grade near the summit.

of Kenosha, Wisconsin, who, legend tells us, had ascended the mountain astride a mule and thereupon vowed to provide a better way for people to get there and back. The story also says that when he made the trip he wore his customary Prince Albert coat and high silk hat. Be that as it may, he was a man of wealth, having made a fortune building telegraph lines and in other business ventures, and today millions of people sleep on Simmons mattresses. He financed the road's construction and until 1925 he or his heirs were the sole owners of the road.

The survey was begun early in April 1889, but was delayed by heavy snows. Grading began not at the bottom, but at the top, and when the line was completed it was found to be only four and one-half feet shorter than the original estimate. Contrary to what one might expect, construction was more difficult and costly in the lowest three miles, where the steep and restless slopes of Engelmann Canyon were harder to conquer than the barren rocks of the higher elevations. In fact, the first three miles above Manitou cost as much to grade as the top six miles. Because of the impossibility of using horses or mules in the grading, all the work was done with pick, shovel and wheelbarrow. The lack of sufficient oxygen at the higher levels made it very difficult for the laborers, and also for the contractors, who had to replace the workmen who deserted the job in droves. Top wages were 25 cents an hour, common labor 18 cents. Six deaths were charged to the construction, two of heart failure, three as the result of blasting, and one man was crushed by a falling boulder.

7

A train on the Half Way House siding in the 1890's, before the engines and cars carried numbers instead of names. — STATE HISTORICAL SOCIETY OF COLORADO

Track laying was completed in four months, ending with the driving of the last spike on October 22, 1890, just 13 months after the grading had begun. Severe electrical disturbances are common on Pike's Peak, and it was often found necessary to insulate the handles of wrenches and other tools with rubber hose.

Train service as far as the Half Way House (just under three miles) was inaugurated in August 1890, but it was not until June 30, 1891 that the first passenger train reached the summit, carrying the members of the choir of the Highland Christian Church of Denver on a special excursion. It is ironic that two trainloads of officials and VIPs were prevented from having the distinction of being the first passengers to reach the summit because of a rockslide above Windy Point.

Although there were some mechanical difficulties with the three locomotives as first built by the Baldwin Locomotive Works, and some adjustments had to be made in the track, passenger service has continued from that June day in 1891 to the present time, snow permitting. In writing about the early operations, a reporter for the *Denver Times* said that "on the lighter grades the train was as fast as a horsecar, and on the steeper ones it was as slow as a horsecar."

To begin passenger operations, the Cog Road ordered six coaches from the Wason Manufacturing Company. They had large glass windows for a full view of the scenery, and narrow seats upholstered with the familiar railroad plush. The exteriors of the cars were a dark Pullman green, with ornate striping in gold leaf.

You can readily understand that freight traffic has not amounted to much, as there are no settlements along the line and pipeline construction ended years ago. At one time there were small but thriving summer colonies at Minnehaha, Half Way House and Ruxton Park, but with the closing of the watershed by the city of Colorado Springs and the increasing use of automobiles, these disappeared. There were hotels of sorts at Minnehaha, Half Way House, and the summit at the turn of the century, none of which operated as late as 1920.

The Cog Road has always had competition. For years hikers traveled its right-of-way to the summit, an all-day trip for a hardy person. Burros were available in Manitou and at

The first passenger train reached the summit on June 30, 1891, carrying a charter group of church choir singers from Denver. — MRS. FRANK C. MARTIN COLLECTION

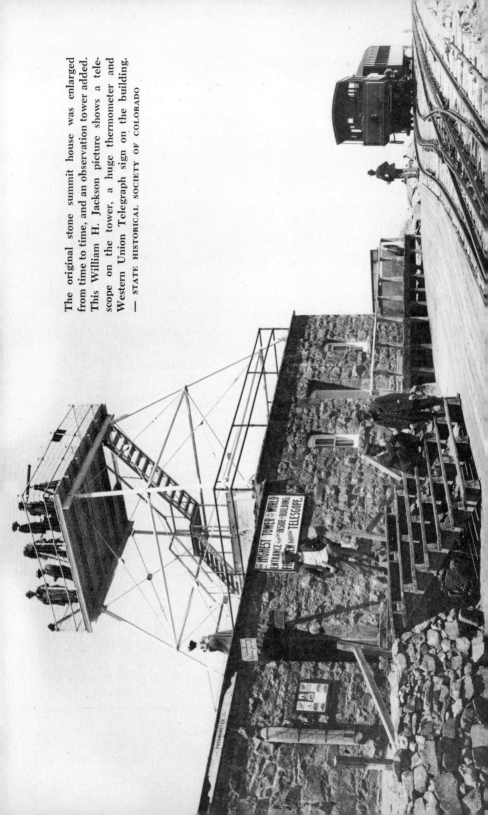

The original stone summit house was enlarged from time to time, and an observation tower added. This William H. Jackson picture shows a telescope on the tower, a huge thermometer and Western Union Telegraph sign on the building. — STATE HISTORICAL SOCIETY OF COLORADO

Before the Cog Road was built, a burro trip was the easiest way to reach the summit. The trail was 12 miles long, a round trip taking most of a day. — DENVER PUBLIC LIBRARY, WESTERN COLLECTION

the upper station of the Mt. Manitou Incline, and that trip was only slightly less arduous than on foot, requiring about 18 hours over the Ruxton trail. Until about 50 years ago a party of tourists would leave Manitou on burros each afternoon, sometimes more than 100 in a party, with several guides or "burro punchers" in attendance. The trail was 12 miles long, and the riders arrived at the summit tired, hungry, perhaps wet and surely half frozen, in time to see the sunrise, clouds permitting. Few of them had ridden anything since hobby-horse days, and the return trip was torture.

In 1883 a toll carriage road was built from Cascade in Ute Pass that reached the summit from the west side. The trip took an entire day, and a more or less thriving business was done hauling tourists, as it was considerably more comfortable than on the back of a mule or burro. In 1915 the Pike's Peak Auto Highway was opened as an improvement over the old carriage road and along much of the old route. An annual event is the Pike's Peak Hill Climb, first run in 1916, when the great Barney Oldfield managed to place twelfth in the field.

11

Between the eras of steam and diesel-electric motive power, the Cog Road designed and built a gasoline-powered single unit, No. 7, shown here at the summit in 1938. It is now retired. — SANBORN PHOTOGRAPH

When steam ruled the mountain, there were seldom more than five or six trains daily, each with a maximum of 50 passengers, but there might be as few as one train and it only partially filled. As the equipment aged and the competition of the automobile and the depression of the 1930's cut down on the patronage, it became obvious that some way had to be found to carry the smaller groups of passengers at less expense.

With this in mind, the company in 1938 designed and built in its Manitou shops a railcar powered by a General Motors gasoline engine. It cost $17,000, seated 24 people and was manned by a crew of only two instead of four men. Its success led to the placing of an order with the General Electric Company for the first of five diesel-electric locomotives that could push a loaded coach carrying a few more passengers than the old cars. They required a crew of four, but resulted in other economies and came at a time when business was recovering from the depression. The gasoline car (No. 7) was then retired. The coaches for these diesel-electrics were built in Denver and featured large glass areas for better viewing of the scenery.

PIKE'S PEAK

MANITOU AND
COG WHEEL ROUTE
PIKE'S PEAK RAILWAY

...Do Not Miss It...

The TRIP of a LIFE TIME

The Grandest Scenery on the Globe

ROUND TRIP IN 4 HOURS.

Low Rate Excursions for the N. E. A.

2 P. M. JULY 7, 9, 11, 13, 14, 15, 17, 19 & 21.

ASK PRINCIPAL RAILWAY TICKET AGENTS ABOUT IT

H. S. CABLE, Pres. and Mgr.
Manitou, Colo.

A very early poster of the Manitou & Pike's Peak Railway, dating from about 1895 and showing the rocky desolation of the line above timberline. — AUTHOR'S COLLECTION

As a result of the economies of these new trains, the steam locomotives disappeared one by one, until in September 1958 the last train to be powered by steam made the round trip with a special charter party. After plowing snow to open the road for traffic in the spring of 1961, No. 4, the last of the steamers, was put in mothballs. In 1968 the management donated it to the Colorado Railroad Museum in Golden, Colorado, where it is now on display.

While the increase in business was welcome, costs continued to rise, so thought was given to something more efficient. In Switzerland, where cog railways are numerous and profitable, most of them operate single-unit cars powered by electricity from overhead wires. To convert the Pike's Peak cog road to electricity would have required an excessive capital investment. Instead, the management contracted for two single-unit diesel-electric rail cars to be made by the Swiss Locomotive Works in Winterthur, Switzerland. These went into service in 1964 and were so satisfactory that two more were ordered and now operate along with the older diesel-electric trains.

Each railcar seats 80 passengers, which means that two of them carry more passengers than three of the older ones, with attendant reduction in overhead. On busy days in the summer tourist season, it is not uncommon for the management to run as many as sixteen trains a day, using both types of equipment. The forward-looking men who direct the company expect to acquire even more advanced models in the future.

The company has consistently striven for improvements in service and efficiency in operation. Continuing this policy, the Manitou & Pike's Peak Railway Company ordered two new diesel trains of revolutionary design in 1973. Built by the Swiss Locomotive & Machine Works, the makers of the four Swiss rail cars already in operation, the new trains each consist of two articulated cars, with a seating capacity of 216 passengers per double-unit. These trains are the first articulated trains in the world to be used on a rack railway. They are powered by four American-made Cummins diesel-hydraulic engines with a combined power output of 1,200

Inaugurating the modern era, the Cog Road began in 1963 to use two new diesel-electric railcars built in Switzerland. These are railcars Nos. 14 and 15. With aspen trees turning a bright golden color, diesel railcar No. 15 passes through Ruxton Park. — SWISS LOCOMOTIVE WORKS (BELOW) One of the new two-car articulated train sets begins to climb the Big Hill shortly after the first official trip to the summit on May 24, 1976. — MANITOU & PIKE'S PEAK RAILWAY

This is a view of the old summit house, with the first diesel-electric train, No. 8 arriving. It shows clearly the rack or cog rails in the center of the track, without which the trains could not climb the steep mountain grade. — GERALD M. BEST

horsepower per train. The first of the two new twin-unit railcars made the official trip to the summit of Pike's Peak on May 24, 1976.

Before their arrival, new passing tracks will be installed, which will eliminate most of the delays that occur at times of heavy traffic on the road. The switches leading to them will be remotely controlled by electricity.

The novel design of the track is one of the more interesting features of the Manitou & Pike's Peak Railway. Operation is by means of rack and pinion, which means that a toothed wheel (pinion) under the locomotive (or car) engages a similarly toothed steel bar (rack) in the center of the track. The layman calls a pinion a cog wheel, and a rack is simply "the cogs." The rack forms a sort of ladder up which the train climbs. Power is furnished by a steam engine, diesel-electric, or electric motor. Without the cog wheel and rack, the wheels would spin and no headway would result, as when an automobile's wheels spin on ice.

16

The very first cog railway in the world was designed and built by Sylvester Marsh, a retired Chicago meat packer, to climb to the top of Mount Washington in New Hampshire. It opened for business in 1869 and is still operating successfully, using steam power.

The scene quickly shifted to the Swiss Alps, where Nicklaus Riggenbach, working independently of Marsh, had designed a cog railway for Mount Rigi that was very similar to Marsh's. That road began operations in 1871 and was soon followed by others.

Both Marsh and Riggenbach used a rack that resembled a narrow, steel ladder, whose rungs provided a foothold for the cog wheels under the engines and cars. Another Swiss, Dr. Roman Abt, designed an improved rack, which is the one used today on the Manitou & Pike's Peak Railway and on a number of others worldwide.

The Abt System calls for two or more parallel rack bars, and cog wheels consisting of a corresponding number of toothed discs to mesh with them. The advantage is that several teeth of the pinion cog wheel can be in contact with the rack simultaneously, making for a smoother action and great safety. Other important systems are the Strub and Locher.

The Abt System of rack rail is well illustrated here. The two racks are securely bolted together and firmly held to the tie. Care in preserving their alignment to a great extent accounts for the safety record of the Cog Road. — AUTHOR'S PHOTO

17

The Big Hill is the longest steep grade on the line, and here we see diesel-electric No. 8 with coach No. 11. In the background is Mt. Almagre, about 2,100 feet lower than Pike's Peak.

— MANITOU & PIKE'S PEAK RAILWAY

This close-up view of the cog wheel and rack under a steam locomotive shows the very sturdy construction of these most important parts, which form a sort of ladder for climbing. The corrugations are on the hand-brake drums, used ordinarily only after stopping. — AUTHOR'S PHOTO

The track is standard gauge (i.e., 4 feet 8½ inches between the rails), with steel rails weighing 40 pounds per yard, which is relatively light as compared with most railroads. To prevent slippage of the track on the steep grades, track anchors were imbedded in rock or gravel every 200 to 600 feet, depending upon the grade. The entire roadbed is on solid ground, none of it on trestles, though there are four short bridges below the site of the Half Way House. Short spur sidings are located at Minnehaha, Mountain View and Windy Point, to allow for the passing of trains.

The gradient of the Cog Road out on the line ranges from a minimum of about six percent to a maximum of 25 percent, which means that the roadbed rises 25 feet vertically for each 100 feet it progresses horizontally. On a 25 percent grade, the upper end of one of the Swiss railcars is about 12 feet higher than its lower end.

The three original steam locomotives were built in 1890 by the Baldwin Locomotive Works in Philadelphia. Each had three cog wheels to provide traction, and the wheels which would otherwise be drive wheels on a regular engine were loose on their axles and served only to support the weight of the locomotive and guide it. These three were originally named *John Hulbert, Manitou* and *Pike's Peak,* but later were numbered 1, 2 and 3 respectively. They were of the type called "simple," which means that they used the expansive power of the steam only once. In order to get more power, they were geared down, which made them rather slow.

In order that their boilers might be fairly level on the steep grades, they were so designed as to maintain that position on a grade of 16 percent, the average of the road. On a level track, as at the Manitou Springs depot, they looked as though they were nosing downhill. The seats of the coaches were similarly tilted, so that the passengers sat more or less upright on the grades.

Steam locomotive *Manitou*, later No. 2, as it looked in 1891. — STATE HISTORICAL SOCIETY OF COLORADO (RIGHT) Engine *Pike's Peak*, later No. 3, stands on the main line at the Half Way House siding, the engineer posing with his traditional symbol of office, the long-spouted oil can. — C. F. MATHEWS COLLECTION

A photograph of the first engine to carry No. 4 on the locomotive roster. This engine met a sad end by running away
in 1896. Nobody was even injured. This dramatic pose against
the sky was used on thousands of post cards. — COLORADO
SPRINGS PUBLIC LIBRARY

Steam locomotive No. 6 was the first and only Cog Road
engine built to burn oil instead of coal, but after one season
was converted to coal burning in 1907. — AUTHOR'S COLLECTION

In the waning days of steam motive power, No. 6 starts up from Manitou, with plenty of smoke, and with steam spurting from its cylinders. In the background, one of the new diesel trains is being unloaded. — BERT WARD

As first built, these engines were not entirely satisfactory, and in 1892 they were rebuilt by Baldwin as Vauclain Compounds. They were followed by four more locomotives, all with minor variations. No. 6, for instance, started as an oil burner, but was soon converted to burn coal, doubtless because the use of oil as a locomotive fuel was then a new and imperfect process.

The locomotives were coaled and watered at Manitou and were then ready for a round trip, with the fireman breaking his back shoveling to keep up the steam pressure. Water was carried in two rather small tanks on the locomotive, and it was necessary to take on more water three times on the way up. The trip with steam power took considerably longer than with the modern power.

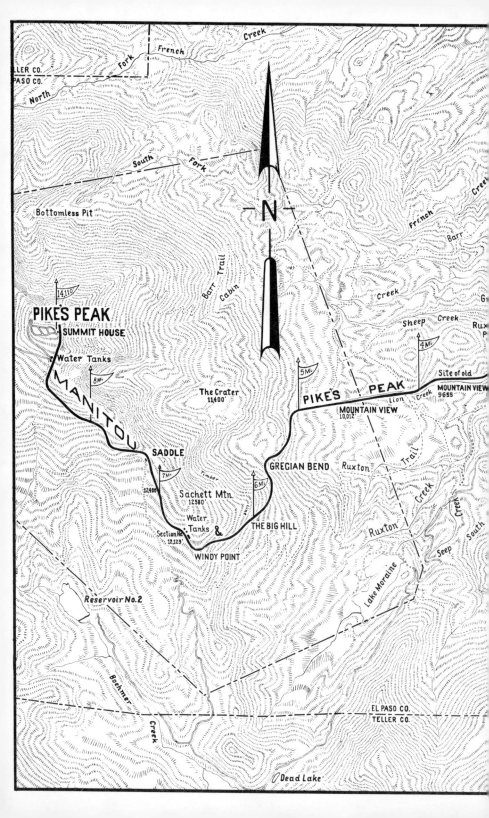

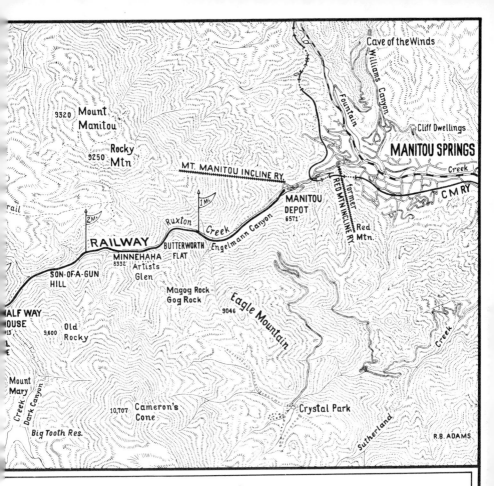

Cave of the Winds

9320 Mount Manitou

Rocky
9250 Mtn

MT. MANITOU INCLINE RY.

Cliff Dwellings

MANITOU SPRINGS

Creek

1 Mi.

Trail

2 Mi.

Ruxton Creek

former RED MTN INCLINE RY.

RAILWAY

BUTTERWORTH FLAT

Engelmann Canyon

MANITOU DEPOT 6571

Williams Canyon

Fountain

C M RY

MINNEHAHA 8332 Artists
Glen

SON-OF-A-GUN HILL

Red Mtn.

Creek

Magog Rock
Gog Rock

9046 Eagle Mountain

HALF WAY HOUSE
913'

9,600 Old Rocky

Creek

Mount Mary

Creek

Dark Canyon

10,707 Cameron's Cone

Crystal Park

Sutherland

R.B. ADAMS

Big Tooth Res.

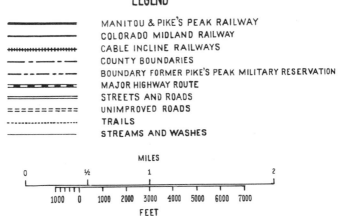

MANITOU & PIKE'S PEAK RAILWAY

LEGEND

———————— MANITOU & PIKE'S PEAK RAILWAY
———————— COLORADO MIDLAND RAILWAY
+++++++++++++ CABLE INCLINE RAILWAYS
— — — — COUNTY BOUNDARIES
— — — — BOUNDARY FORMER PIKE'S PEAK MILITARY RESERVATION
———————— MAJOR HIGHWAY ROUTE
———————— STREETS AND ROADS
=========== UNIMPROVED ROADS
···················· TRAILS
———————— STREAMS AND WASHES

MILES

0   ½   1   2

1000   0   1000 2000 3000 4000 5000 6000 7000

FEET

MILEAGE ORIGINALLY MEASURED FROM PIKE'S PEAK

40' CONTOUR LINES EVERY 40'

Engine *Pike's Peak* and coach *Salida* ease down Son-of-a-Gun Hill, a 25 percent grade. Later both locomotive and coach received numbers instead of names, the engine becoming No. 3. — CARL F. MATHEWS COLLECTION

The steam locomotives were not coupled to the coaches, but merely pushed them, and the same applies to the diesel-electric trains today. Descending, the speed of the train was controlled by the engineer, with some help from the brakeman on the coach. Though the engines had hand brakes, they were seldom used, and the locomotives descended slowly because air was compressed in the cylinders, allowing them to come down much as an automobile can descend a hill in a lower gear without the use of brakes. The engineer could release this air as he wished — slowly to retard speed, faster to pick up speed.

The original wooden coaches, of which there were six, were named for Colorado towns and cities — *Denver, Aspen, Cripple Creek, Salida, Colorado Springs,* and *Leadville.* In later years they were numbered 101 through 106 and the names were dropped. They were built with only four wheels and a wheelbase of 20 feet 6 inches, which proved to be too long for the curves; hence, they were soon fitted with four-wheel trucks, one at each end.

Each coach had two independent sets of hand brakes, and both could be applied from either platform. In those days a brakeman stood at a brake wheel at all times, and if necessary he could apply the brakes and stop the car within a few feet. A similar procedure is followed on the modern trains for the sake of safety.

It had been planned originally that one engine would push two cars, which is why they ordered six coaches for three locomotives. As it turned out, the engines did not have enough power to do this, and always a train consisted of one coach and one engine. A seventh coach was built in 1906, which was too heavy and was seldom used. Only one of these cars remains, and it is used for storage purposes.

The modern Swiss railcars have every known and improved type of safety feature; they have also been free of accidents. In fact, the road has maintained an enviable safety record in its more than 80 years of operation.

Nature's bounty in the Pike's Peak region often includes more than an ample endowment of snow. White-capped Pike's Peak, standing like a giant overlord, adds a full measure of scenic beauty to the countryside. But snow is no blessing to railroaders, though loved by photographers and ski buffs.

At high elevations it can be winter in summer, and in spring and autumn this can cause serious problems. While there have been years when it was possible to open the road in late March with little trouble, it usually doesn't pay, as a fall of several feet of snow the following week is apt to close the line and make a second plowing necessary. Besides, there are few tourists who want to make the trip that early. Therefore, the Cog Road usually opens May 1st and closes in late October, the dates depending upon the amount of snow and the demand for tickets.

While the ordinary railroad snowplow is a huge wedge that splits the snow right and left, such a plow cannot be used on the Manitou & Pike's Peak, for the reason that one side or the other of the track is always up against the mountainside. Furthermore, the speed necessary for such a plow is impossible to attain. Instead, a flat wedge is used to ram under the snow,

27

Working above timberline, the steam locomotive and flatcar-plow struggled in 1905 to clear the line, a job not enjoyed by the section crews. — GRANT G. SIMMONS SR. COLLECTION

which is thus automatically loaded onto a flat car. After dropping down the hill to an open space, this load of snow is dumped off to one side of the track by tilting the car bed. Then, back for another go at it. The road also has a rotary plow that was built in its own shops, which is useful for lighter snow, but is inclined to have difficulty with ice or snow that is hard packed.

The worst year for snow in recent times was in 1969, when the opening was late and the closing early. On June 28 of that year, there were drifts five to seven feet deep, and in October, when the average snowfall is about seven inches, there were 70 inches at Ruxton Park and at the summit.

"Springtime in the Rockies." After a light snowfall, passengers aboard No. 9 mingle with snow shovelers at the summit of Pike's Peak. BOB MCINTYRE (BELOW) The rotary snowplow, No. 21, was designed and built in the Cog Road's own shops. In this scene at Mountain View, trainmen check out a malfunction. — MANITOU & PIKE'S PEAK RAILWAY

In the 1890's, Wm. H. Jackson photographed this excellent view of the lower terminal of the Cog Road. At the left is the Iron Springs Hotel, the depot is in the center, and the shops and train shed are at the lower right. — STATE HISTORICAL SOCIETY OF COLORADO

Officially, at various times, the town has been called either Manitou or Manitou Springs, and currently is the latter. At the mouth of Engelmann Canyon and close to the famous old Ute Iron Spring, stand the depot, shops, and operating headquarters of the Manitou & Pike's Peak Railway. From this point all trains leave for the summit of Pike's Peak.

Here also are the storage sheds for the rolling stock, which include a flat car that doubles as a snow plow, the rotary plow, and a gasoline powered work car that carries the section crew and supplies up the line as needed.

Retired engine No. 5 is on display at the end of track, and could possibly be put back into shape to run again, though this is highly improbable. Other steam locomotives are on display in Manitou Springs, at the Cheyenne Mountain Zoo in Colorado Springs, and at the Colorado Railroad Museum in Golden.

In the years when automobiles were non-existent, few in number, or lacking in ability, practically all the prospective passengers came from Colorado Springs on the electric interurban cars. To carry them on from the end of that line to the Cog Road depot, there was a short electric trolley which, be-

In the horse-and-buggy days, passengers arrived at the Manitou depot of the Cog Road in hired conveyances, including surreys. The building is essentially unchanged today. — MANITOU & PIKE'S PEAK RAILWAY

Coach No. 106, photographed at the depot, was the last of the cars built for use with steam locomotives. Being too heavy for the engines to push, it ended its days on the ground as a shelter at Mountain View. — STATE HISTORICAL SOCIETY OF COLORADO

This little four-wheeled trolley, one of two, carried passengers from the center of Manitou up to the Cog Road depot. It was locally referred to as *the Dinky*. — S. D. MAGUIRE COLLECTION

Built in 1908, the Mt. Manitou Incline's lower station is opposite that of the Cog Road. The Incline offers a wonderful view of the plains and cities to the east. This scene dates back some 60 years. The maximum gradient is 68 percent, more than 2.5 times that of the Cog Road. — STEWARTS COMMERCIAL PHOTOGRAPHERS

cause of its stubby four-wheeled cars, was called the *Dinky*. Two cars were used in summer, and they met and passed at the half-way point. Shuttling back and forth as fast as they could, they ferried all the passengers to the cog depot. In fact, the Cog Road's trains operated and still do on the same principle — they run as often and as long as traffic requires.

Opposite the depot is the lower terminal of the Mt. Manitou Incline Railway, a cable or funicular operating on the slopes of Mt. Manitou. This line has been in successful operation since 1908, ascending to where an excellent view may be had of the plains to the east. The railway is one mile long, rising some 2,000 feet in that distance, with a maximum gradient of 68 percent. The ownership is the same as the Manitou & Pike's Peak Railway, and it is the longest and highest incline cable road in the country.

Manitou Springs, where the lower station of the Cog Road is located, lies close to the mountains at an elevation of 6,570 feet. This is at the foot of Engelmann Canyon, which was so named because of the profusion of Engelmann spruce trees that grow on its steep slopes. Both Manitou Springs and nearby Colorado Springs were founded in 1872 by promoters of the Denver & Rio Grande Railroad.

Along the Cog Railway . . .

Because the track follows Ruxton Creek up this narrow canyon, the view is restricted for the first three miles to relatively nearby scenes, but these are both beautiful and interesting. Huge boulders abound, some in unusual positions or shapes. Among them are Gog and Magog, named for the Biblical giants, Jumbo the Elephant Rock, the Ace of Diamonds, and Hanging Rock. Soon after negotiating a bit of 25 percent grade, the train comes to Minnehaha, which in years past was a summer colony and headquarters of the Alpine Botanical Laboratory for the study of alpine flora. A section house and water tank were also here, and a few hundred yards farther along we come to Son-of-a-Gun Hill, another grade of 25 percent, whose name so shocked some Victorians that they spelled it Sun-of-a-Gun.

Early in 1938, engine No. 3 leaves the Manitou station for the nine-mile run to the summit of Pike's Peak with coach No. 101. Since then, new coach sheds and additional tracks have been built here. — RICHARD B. JACKSON

Just above the Manitou depot, engine No. 2 pushes a train through Engelmann Canyon. The track to the right of the train leads down into the company shops. — R. H. KINDIG COLLECTION (BELOW) Leaving Engelmann Canyon, this train in 1891 approaches Minnehaha, which was a small summer colony years ago. Note the view of the plains in the background. — HEISTAND PHOTO, AUTHOR'S COLLECTION

The log Half Way House, a popular summer hotel, predated the Cog Road by several years. It was finally dismantled in 1926 after standing idle for a few years. — AUTHOR'S COLLECTION

Then comes the site of the old Half Way House, which for some 40 years was a popular summer resort hotel. It was built of logs, and over the course of years from 1882 had grown from a single room to perhaps 15 bedrooms, a main room, dining room, and kitchen. It did have electricity, but the only running water was through a pipe from South Ruxton Creek to the kitchen, and the only heat was from the fireplaces in the main room and dining room, and the kitchen range. Experienced guests took a hotwater bottle to bed with them to keep their feet warm and to furnish tepid water for face washing in the morning. Room and board in the early 1900's cost

$10 a week. A stable of burros supplied mounts for those who would ride to Pike's Peak or elsewhere, and attracted armies of flies.

The Half Way House depot was also a summer post office and souvenir stand. Mail came up six days a week from Manitou on a mule, but service ended with the tourist season. In spite of the name, the place was only about one-third of the distance to the summit and one-third of the rise, and many a hiker turned back on learning that he wasn't half way at all.

The Half Way House depot-post office-curio stand as it was through the early 1900's. The main line climbs to the right, the siding goes off to the left. The man who seems to be sitting in the middle of the track is riding a track toboggan used by employees for fast descent. — TUTT LIBRARY, COLORADO COLLEGE

Just above the Half Way House (of which nothing remains today) at an elevation of just over 9,000 feet is Ruxton Park, which was once a townsite whose lots were often more vertical than horizontal. Now we begin to see more distant scenes. Ahead of the train is Mt. Almagre, which at first glance looks like Pike's Peak. It is well above timberline, but is about 2,100 feet lower than the peak.

A curve to the right at Pilot Knob (on the left) brings into view the majestic mass of Pike's Peak, which emphasizes the

The train in this breathtaking scene of the 1890's has just passed through Hell Gate and stands at Ruxton Park. Mt. Almagre, not Pike's Peak, may be seen in the background. — HIESTAND PHOTO, AUTHOR'S COLLECTION

Pike's Peak forms a magnificent backdrop for the former office of *The Pike's Peak Daily News* at Mountain View. Just above here all steam locomotives took on water for the climb up the Big Hill. — STATE HISTORICAL SOCIETY OF COLORADO

enormity of the engineering problems that beset but did not defeat the builders of the Cog Road back in 1889-90. Along here the track seems to be almost level and the train moves faster, yet the gradient ranges from eight to ten percent.

Approaching Mountain View, where the old steamers stopped for water before attacking the Big Hill, is the longest bit of straight track (or tangent) on the entire line, some 4,000 feet. For many of the early years, *The Pike's Peak Daily News* was published here. Most of it was preprinted, and while the train went on to the top and back an insert was run off on a small press. This insert contained the names and addresses

A steam powered cog train gets up steam for the 25 percent gradient of the Big Hill. The new diesel-electric trains of today hardly notice it! — BERT WARD COLLECTION

of the passengers, most of whom were glad to pay a quarter for a copy to take home and show the neighbors.

Above Mountain View the grade gradually increases and, after rounding a few curves, we begin the long and arduous climb up the Big Hill. In the days of steam power it was often necessary for the train to halt on the steepest part in order to let the engine get up enough steam to keep going. In fact, the fireman spent most of his time heaving coal into the firebox, and as a rule shoveled a ton of it on the trip up.

It is on the Big Hill that we notice a marked change in the vegetation. The aspens and pines are left behind us and only

39

Smoking up the Big Hill, above timberline and not far below Windy Point, with a beautiful view of Lake Moraine far below. This is a semi-artificial lake used as a reservoir of the Colorado Springs Water System. Ruxton Creek flows from it and down to Ruxton Park, where most of the water is conducted by pipe to Mt. Manitou and down to a power plant near the Cog Road depot. — BERT WARD COLLECTION

On the Big Hill at timberline, which is approximately 12,000 feet above sea level. The grade at this point is 25 percent.
— GERALD M. BEST

spruce trees, small shrubs and grasses grow. As we approach timberline most of the trees appear stunted and some have limbs only on one side of the trunk, testifying to the strength and persistance of the wind. And then, at about 12,000 feet, there are no more trees or shrubs. Along with the grasses, many dwarf flowering plants abound wherever there is a little soil between the rocks. In a very short season they must bloom and produce seeds.

As we climb the Big Hill, it becomes apparent that what looked like huge mountains from Manitou have shrunk in stature when viewed from above. Lake Moraine and the Seven Lakes become visible far below us. They are semi-artificial lakes that form a part of the water system of Colorado Springs. Usually a train or two will be in sight on the track below us, steadily crawling up the steep slope.

Rounding a shoulder of the mountain, the track passes through a shallow cut through the rock (the only cut on the road) and we are at Windy Point. By this time the passengers feel the cold and close the windows. In the olden days of steam, the conductors were permitted to add to their meager incomes by renting overcoats to the thoughtless and shivering tourists at two bits a throw, and each conductor had his own collection of secondhand coats of all sizes and colors.

Beside the track on the right are the old stone section house, not used these many years, the old water tank and, across the track, a siding. Soon those on the right side of the

This is the type of desolation that prevails on the higher slopes, where only alpine plants and grasses grow. The old steam train in this view is beginning the last climb to the summit. — BERT WARD COLLECTION

car will be able to get a very brief view of the plains out to the east as we pass the Saddle, and from here a few minutes bring us to the top of Pike's Peak, 14,110 feet above sea level and 7,500 feet above the lower station in Manitou, which we have climbed in 8.9 miles of track.

As we sit in our comfortable coach, we must not forget that the weather on this mountain can change very quickly from sunshine to sleet and snow. On a day in August 1911, a man and his wife froze to death beside the track only about half a mile below the summit house, having disregarded warnings

43

Diesel train No. 8, the first of the diesel-electrics, approaches the summit during its first year of operation. Seven Lakes and the plains are visible in the distance. At this time the train was aluminum in color with a decorative red trim. — R. H. KINDIG

and being lightly clothed. In the man's pocket was found a post card from a friend, closing with the words, "Have a good time, and don't freeze to death on Pike's Peak."

From the summit we can see to the east into Kansas, and in the opposite direction the once booming gold camps of Cripple Creek and Victor are only a few miles away. Farther away are the peaks of the Continental Divide, including Mt. Elbert, the highest in Colorado (14,433 feet above the sea). To the north are other peaks of the Front Range and the great city of Denver, while Pueblo is to the south, and beyond that the Sangre de Cristo range of mountains.

Just beyond the end of the track is a sight well worth the short walk — Bottomless Pit. Actually it is a drop of about 2,300 feet to its floor, where there was once a gold mine but no gold.

At the end-of-track, on the summit, is a sheer drop of some 2,300 feet into Bottomless Pit. One edge of it is shown here in this view from the automobile road. — STEWARTS COMMERCIAL PHOTOGRAPHERS

The very modern summit house was opened in 1964, succeeding an old stone building that began as a weather station in 1871 and had been enlarged and used by the Cog Road as its terminal. Here, a few feet below the exposed surface rocks, is permafrost, ice that never melts. At this altitude water boils at 184 degrees Fahrenheit, which means that it is impractical to try to boil potatoes or beans, and a boiled egg is a gamble.

In 1906, just north of the summit house, a bronze tablet was unveiled commemorating the discovery of the mountain by Lt. Zebulon Pike a century earlier. For years there was also a wooden headboard marking the last resting place of Erin O'Keefe, daughter of Sgt. O'Keefe of the U.S. Signal

The new summit house, opened in 1964, is a great improvement over the old structure, but by no means as photogenic. Old timers miss the stone work and the tower of the old building. The summit house is used by both railway and auto road visitors. — STEWARTS COMMERCIAL PHOTOGRAPHERS

One of the first of four Swiss railcars, painted in fire engine red livery, discharges its passengers at the summit of Pike's Peak. — MANITOU & PIKE'S PEAK RAILWAY

Service, who was eaten by mountain rats in the old summit house in 1876. This was pure malarky, one of the tall tales concocted by the sergeant to while away the time, for he had no daughter and wasn't even married. But O'Keefe did have a pet cat named Erin, which he is said to have buried with full military honors.

The return trip is just as full of interest as was the trip up, and we see things we missed before. Families of marmots or "whistle pigs" sun themselves on the rocks and whistle at the train as it passes. Quite often small bands of mountain sheep or bighorns can be seen grazing on the sparse grass of the high pasture, and deer are fairly common. There are plenty of ground squirrels and chipmunks, and a number of different species of birds from jays to ravens.